Emma Elizabeth Brown

Huldah

A Daughter of the Revolution and other Poems of American Patriotism

Emma Elizabeth Brown

Huldah
A Daughter of the Revolution and other Poems of American Patriotism

ISBN/EAN: 9783337307219

Printed in Europe, USA, Canada, Australia, Japan

Cover: Foto ©Thomas Meinert / pixelio.de

More available books at **www.hansebooks.com**

HULDAH

A DAUGHTER OF THE REVOLUTION

AND OTHER

POEMS OF AMERICAN PATRIOTISM

EMMA E. BROWN

———

BOSTON
LOTHROP PUBLISHING COMPANY

TO

L. A. B.

OF THE

D. A. R.

THESE POEMS OF AMERICAN PATRIOTISM
ARE AFFECTIONATELY INSCRIBED

BY

E. E. B.

CONTENTS

HULDAH

HULDAH

A DAUGHTER OF THE REVOLUTION

———————

Low, subtle whispers of summer-
    tide,
Though fringes of snow still clung
    beside
The jagged rocks, and with half-
    dazed look —
Like a child just waked — lay the
    sleepy brook.
Perchance 'twas the sunshine's length-
    ened ray,
The lowing cattle, the haze that lay
On the Milton hills, or that strange
    spell
In the robin's note — I cannot
    tell —
But Huldah leaving her spinning,
    knew
And felt the restlessness as she
    threw

9 ·

The bars of the lattice open. Cool
    and sweet
As though from some pine wood's
    deep retreat —
With a slow, coy tread, the fresh
    winds crept
Through the sliding bars ; on the
    hearth, wing-swept,
Falls the startled log in a moulder-
    ing heap,
While with playful touch the breezes
    keep
The dried bouquets on the mantel-
    shelves
In trembling rustle ; like roguish elves
At hide and seek 'mongst the piles
    of wool
Soft-carded, with sudden start they
    pull
And twist the thread on the idle
    wheel,
Tumble the curls of Huldah, and
    steal
Across her cheeks to leave a flush,
Borrowed, it may be, from the blush
Of pink arbutus, anemones,
In their out-door work of mysteries.

Then, planning fresh mischief, the
    rude winds stray
To the pantry where ('tis Saturday),
The brown bread moulding with busy
    hands,
By her kneading-trough the mother
    stands ;
Another gust — away flies her cap !
And tabby starts from a half-feigned
    nap
When fragrant mints from the old
    cross-beam
Drop into the pan of golden cream !

A merry laughing, while swift feet
    run
To close the bars ere more harm is
    done,
And yet by the lattice, a long time
    still
The young girl lingers, as young
    girls will
When the breath of Spring thrills
    heart and brain
With a rapture — half akin to pain !
But green are the buds on the wil-
    lows' bough,

And fragrant the sod where ox and
  plough
The father, in home-spun suit of
  blue,
Is guiding the broad, deep furrows
  through.

A sudden rumble — a quick, bright
  flash
In the April skies! But, closing
  the sash,
Our little Huldah with happy smile
Has turned away, and merrily while
Her wheel is spinning, she sings a
  strain
That seems of her own glad thoughts,
  the refrain:

A sunlit sky and a sunlit earth —
Blue hills and a bluer river, —
Cool forest depths where the springs
  have birth,
Green fields where the grasses quiver!

A fair bright future — without and
  within —
Glad Hope to my heart is bringing,

For a golden thread do the grim Fates
    spin
When they hear — a red-breast sing-
    ing !

————

Another morning — just two hours
    old —
A Sunday morning, clear and cold.
Without, the crest of a waning moon
Is slipping from brow of the Night;
    for, soon,
Swift heralds of Dawn the east will
    rend
And electric flash through the whole
    land send !
Chill breezes from marsh and low-
    lands creep,
Rustling the trees where dead leaves
    sleep ;
And, now and then, through the
    woods is heard
The wandering note of some shiver-
    ing bird.

In the little farm-house all is still
Save the tick of the clock, the shrill

Sharp chirp of cricket, or tramp of mice
'Twixt the loosened laths.
      Hark! twice — ay, thrice!
And again it comes! Good God!
    can it mean —
Nay — hush! there's a cry the swift
    footsteps between, —
An echoing tread on the bridge be-
    low, —
Another call! — and, like startled doe,
Half doubting still if she wakes or
    sleeps
The little Huldah, a-tremble, creeps
Down the creaking stair-case, peers
    without
The great hall door, and catching the
    shout
Of the flying horseman, one dread
    word,
" *The British!* " through all the house
    is heard,
Till the old oak rafters themselves
    are stirred!

To the upper loft the father springs
And forth from its hiding-place he
    brings

The heavy musket that he bore
At Frontenac, long years before.
" The red-coats — ha ! they shall not
　　say
With bullets we know but children's
　　play ! "
And with soldier-pride he soothes
　　the fears
Of wife and of daughter, kisses the
　　tears
Away from Huldah's cheeks, and
　　then
Runs down to the green where the
　　" minute men "
Their quiet hamlet homes to save
Have gathered in phalanx stanch and
　　brave.

Ah — well-a-day ! — you all have
　　heard
That Sabbath's story, — word for
　　word —
How nobly they fought at Lexing-
　　ton, —
The short, sharp conflict farther on,—
The fierce bush fighting — then the
　　shout

Of victory; and the British rout,
As with broken ranks they turned
    and fled —
The proud Lord Percy at their head!
Yet what is our knowledge — thine
    or mine—
Of that one day — save the bare out-
    line!
In Huldah's home — why! the long
    hours crept
As if the very pendulum slept.
The cries of alarm, the gathering feet
Soon died away; but the quiet street,
The dead, dull silence everywhere,
Seemed harder than anything else to
    bear!
For man may fight, but woman must
    wait, —
And which — think you — is the
    easier fate?

There were distant shots, and now
    and then
The smell and the smoke of powder,
    when
With chilling breath, and a wailing
    sound

The fickle winds to the east veered
   round ;
Snug, sheltered, and safe from rude
   alarm
In its quiet nook, stood the hillside
   farm,
Yet the mother and Huldah felt a
   chill
As they looked and listened — a sudden thrill
Of quick, sharp pain — for dearer
   far
Than our own poor lives, our loved
   ones are !
And our very safety — when theirs,
   we know,
In peril must be — is an added woe !

On the upper shelf, at close of day,
Still folded the Sunday garments lay ;
The catechism's dreaded task
The mother had quite forgotten to
   ask,
And now the last red shaft in the
   west
Had ended the hours of sacred rest
For the day was reckoned (as it begun

In the good old times) from sun to
    sun!
And laying aside the Holy Book
Her half-knitted stocking the mother
    took,
While little Huldah began to reel
Fresh skeins of yarn from her spin-
    ning-wheel;
But dull and listless her fingers ply
The wonted stint, though she stands
    close by
The lattice window where field and
    brook
And bud and bough have the self-
    same look
As yester-morn — yet the fairest
    scene
Strange shadows may catch from —
    a day between!

A weeping sky and a mourning earth, —
    Bleak hills and a bleaker river, —
Dark forest wilds where the storms
    have birth, —
    Brown fields where the dead leaves
    shiver;

A dim, gray future — within and with-
out —
Dread Fear to my heart is bringing,
For in the chill dusk, when truth is a
doubt,
I heard — a whip-poor-will singing !

———

With weight of blossom — with fruit-
age now,
Droops the trailing vine and the
loaded bough, —
Through the gray old woods the
flowers have gone
In long procession, one by one;
The trembling snow-drop's pallid
face
Had hardly smiled ere it yielded
place
To violets, to twin-flower bells,
And the sweet claytonia that dwells
A hermit within its mossy nook;
And now, like lighted torch by the
brook,
Flames the cardinal-flower, while
golden rod
And the asters' deep rich purple, nod

In the meadows brown, as if the sun
And shadow were melted into one!

And all this time the tide of war
Whose sudden rise old Middlesex
     saw,
That April morning — as in a
     dream —
Has ebbed and flowed in one vast
     stream
Throughout the land; their white
     and red
The bright June roses scarce had shed,
When on Charlestown's height the
     battle came
That gave to one hill a world-wide
     fame!
Nor do Southern homes their heroes
     lack;
For Patrick Henry echoes back
The same determined will that fired
Our bold Green Mountain boys —
     inspired
Young Ethan Allen, when the " keys
Of Canada " he vowed to seize,
And at Ticonderoga show
How a true soldier meets the foe!

With smaller file, but fiercer heart —
(It may be that the touch, the smart
Of rifle-balls — like some wines make
Fresh thirst, that needs fresh draughts
    to slake !)
Long weeks ago the " minute-men "
To Lexington returning, when
Their service, for the time, was
    through, —
With eager, longing eyes the few
Thin ranks were scanned by one and
    all
Whose homes had heard that " morn-
    ing call."
And while, impatient, to the gate
Our little Huldah runs to wait,
The careful mother — ere it burn —
Her smoking " fire-cake " stops to
    turn,
And lay upon the fresh-scoured deal,
Where waits the simple evening meal,
An extra spoon, knife, fork and
    plate
For " father," for the hour is late,
And hungry, faint, she fears that
    he
After the hard day's march will be.

In long-drawn line the troops pass on,
Till now the scattered files have gone
Far down the road ; and all alone,
With altered step, with altered tone,
Poor Huldah turns, to meet half-way
The mother's sudden, sad dismay —
" And yet 'tis likely we may find
He tarried, just a while, behind —
Or, mayhap, joined the troops that
        lay
Around old Boston, for they said
With Washington now at their head
The ' Continentals' meant, ere long,
To enter in, with shout and song ! "

So Huldah and the mother try
To cheer each other — drawing nigh
The dying embers, as they wait
To hear the footstep at the gate.
And   still   untouched   the   supper
        stands
While steadily the old clock's hands
Are travelling on from hour to hour
As if they held some subtle power,
And knew our hopes, fears, life and
        death
The while they number every breath !

With morning came fresh hope, fresh
    plan —
By questioning each " minute-man "
The truth, of course, would soon be
    shown,
And it were better all were known —
The very worst — than longer bear
This burden of suspense and care.
What did they learn? Well, one
    man said
That he had seen him far ahead
Of rank and file that morning when
The call had come for " minute-
    men ";
Another said, " He fought right
    well —
A very hero — till he fell."

" Fell ? " Huldah's lips grew white
    with fear,
The mother gasped, " We did not
    hear —
We did not know " — " Nay ! don't
    mistake,"
The blunt lips added, " lines must
    break
In fight, you know ; we fall, we rise,

And I am sure these very eyes
Saw the brave man again, ere long
Right in the thickest of the throng!"
"Yes! Up and fighting!" said a
        third,
" He sprang as lightly as a bird
From that first wound." But then
        — what then?
Well, really it was doubtful when
The fierce bush-fighting came, to tell
What happened — some ran on —
        some fell —
And some had tarried to defend
The broken columns at the end;
While others hid in ambush, more,
However, had pressed on before
To hasten the retreat; blockade
The city — they themselves had
        stayed
Most willingly, but calls at home
So urgent grew that they had come
To be "at minute's warning" still
All ready — with a right good will!

With aching heart, word after word,
As in a dream, the mother heard;
And Huldah, as she listened, grew —

(Such sudden change our grief and
pain
Will sometimes work — like summer
rain)
A woman, strong to bear, to do !

———

Amethyst skies, and chrysoprase hills,
Where the lengthening sunbeam creepeth,
Murmur of South winds, babble of
rills,
Whistling of orioles, bob-o-link trills,
Yet soundly the little bud sleepeth.

Dull, leaden skies where the heavy
clouds lower,
Hills the glad sunshine forsaketh,
Raw, piercing winds and a chill,
drenching shower,
Sobbing of pines where the bleating
herds cower,
Yet, look you! the little bud waketh!

———

O dreary winter! Just outside
The city still, the troops abide ;

For though, weeks since, the frozen
    bay
Temptations offered to essay
The promised, long-deferred attack,
Yet wise war councils held them back
A little longer still, till men,
Stores, ammunition came, and then
More confident the raid would be,
And crowned with surer victory ;
So reasoned Washington, and so
The patriots resolved to do.

Meanwhile, young Burr and Arnold
    toil
Through pathless wilds of Maine, to
    spoil
Quebec, and there unite, at length,
To give the New York troops fresh
    strength.
And midst discouragements untold,
Montgomery, with ardor bold,
Showed how a strong will could
    prevail
The " Heights of Abraham " to scale.

On leaden wings the months crept
    on ;

The cold white drifts were almost
    gone,
And through the lattice bars once
    more
Came hints of summer days in store.
One hope, and only one, remained :
If entrance should, at last, be gained
Within the city — who could tell ?
The father might be there — 'tis well
To hope, and Huldah tries to cheer
The mother, and allay her fear,
The while her busy fingers ply
Their daily tasks, and bravely try
By ready work of ready hand
To help the patriotic band.

A single night — and lo ! the sun
Next morning showed more labor
    done
" Than my vast army, I believe,
In a whole month's time could
    achieve ! "
The British general exclaimed —
Of his own laggard troops ashamed.
Eleven days from that March night,
And Boston gloried in the sight
Of streets that knew no more the tread

Of Tory or the royal red!
And while the British fleet still lay
At anchor, just outside the bay,
A new, strange banner met their
    eyes
Of thirteen stripes against the skies!

From our own grief and misery
Springs the sweet balm of sympathy;
And burdened souls, because they
    know
Life's bitterness, are quick to show
That Christian charity which is
So rare in such a world as this!
And when the thought had come,
    that he —
The lost one — 'mongst the sick
    might be,
Though never word, trace, sight or
    sound
Of their own loved one could be
    found,
Yet hearing there the piteous cries
Of one poor sufferer, who lies
Just at Death's door — what do they
    care
Though British uniform he wear?

With soothing words, with gentle
touch
That to the sick one means so much,
The mother's tender, loving hand
His burning cheeks and forehead
fanned ;
Brought dainty bits from off her
shelf —
Delicious comfits she herself
From luscious fruits prepared as no
One else (the father said) could do !
And when the soldier, half awake,
(He came from Devonshire, it seemed,
And of his English home had
dreamed)
From long delirium cried, " Oh !
take
Me quick away ! I long to see
The sparkling brook, the old oak
tree,
The fresh green fields, the woods,
the pond,
And those blue mountains just be-
yond ! " —
The mother said, " Why ! let him
come
To us — we have a country home,

And room to spáre — the change
    might do
More for him than the doctors
    knew ! "

And so it happened, one bright day
Within their little guest-room, lay
A British soldier ! And the news
A wondrous zeal and fire infuse;
But when the noble women hear
The innuendoes, taunt and jeer —
The epithets of " Tory," " Spy," —
To one and all they make reply,
" 'Tis surely but a simple deed
Of charity, as, in his need,
We would some pitying heart and
    true
For our belovèd one might do ! "

———

I had a message for my love,
   Full tender, deep, and true ;
And yet, O waiting, white-winged dove
   I could not give it you !

A fresh breeze kissed my cheek, —
   It passed unto the South —

The land that all my longings seek —
  Yet sealèd was my mouth.

The good ship touched the shore,
  She sailed far out of ken,
And yet no messages she bore,
  No words of tongue or pen.

Just then, across my path
  A sudden shadow came,
One of God's poor, who hath
  The blessing, " in His name,"

One for whom Jesu died
  Had fallen by the road;
I could not turn aside —
  I gave him raiment, food,

And words of friendly cheer —
  Who could do less than this
For one, a fellow man, whose tear,
  Whose smile reflecteth his ?

Yet suddenly there shone
  The light of a new day;
The message had passed on
  In God's own blessèd way !

For Love is still the same —
　Whate'er we dream or think —
Though bound to one fond name,
　Perchance, yet many a link

The magic chain must make,
　Ere heart can answer heart
In perfect concord, and thus take
　Of heaven's own joy a part!

———

Now at the North — now at the
　South —
The demon War, with half-closed
　mouth,
Had muttered challenges all through
The Spring; and many knew
The British Parliament had vowed
"This rebel handful" should be
　cowed
At once, if force of arms and men
Could bring obedience back again.
But when Sir Peter's boasted strength
Before old Moultrie, quailed, at
　length;
And Clinton's bold attempts were
　foiled

At Charleston, till his ships were
    spoiled
Of colors, ammunition, stores —
Grave apprehensions filled the corps
Of " British regulars " ; and now
Though troops had come from Ad-
    miral Howe,
And though the feeble patriot band
Was suffering loss, on sea, on land —
Behold ! a tremor shakes the throne
Of monarchs — wheresoever known,
As Declaration — loud and clear —
Of Independence, greets the ear !
And a new Nation takes her stand
United — heart and soul and hand.
A race full-grown, full-armed, in-
    deed —
As in old classic lore we read
How the prolific brain of Zeus
A perfect Pallas could produce ;
And how a legion on the plain
Of Thebes arose, from dragon slain !

But ah ! not yet may conflict cease —
Since armor is for war, not peace —
And Liberty so dear, so rare,
The precious seal of blood must bear.

Now at Long Island — at White
     Plains —
With many losses, many gains,
The contest rages fierce and strong,
While shouts of victory belong,
Now to the royal flag, and now
To bars and stars, whose colors show
The heavens above, the stripes below !

With eager ear that autumn day,
The British soldier as he lay
Half-sleeping, half-awake, had heard
The neighbors when they brought
     the word
To Huldah — tarrying the while
To catch the sunshine of her smile.

A crow's sharp " caw," and plaintive
     note
Of "pewee" through the still air float,
And from the purpling grapes, a
     breath
(Like that the sweet day-lily hath)
Comes through the open sash ; and
     now
A red leaf from the maple bough
Has dropped upon the sill ; a bee

All honey-laden, and a free
Bright butterfly flit in and out;
And from the orchard comes the
    shout
Of children as they shake the loaded
    tree.

O rich, ingathering time! The earth
In springtide, to maintain the birth
Of myriad buds, perforce must drain
The air of stimulus; and brain,
Breath, muscle, feel in turn the need
Of life absorbed by germ and seed.
But autumn comes with garnered
    store, —
The teeming earth o'erflows once
    more, —
And clasping her full hand we take
The quick, magnetic thrills that make
It bliss to breathe — ay! ecstasy
As in our childhood — just to be!

And so that bright October day
While listlessly the sick man lay
And let his thoughts in quiet rhythm
Blend with the scene — a sudden
    chrism

Seemed falling on him as the dew,
And every nerve, vein, fibre, knew
The tide had turned — the open door
Of life, not death, was his once more.
He glanced about him, raised his head,
And as he caught the busy tread
Of feet below, and then the song
Of Huldah at her work, a throng
Of happy thoughts filled heart and
    brain
And love of life crept back again.

SONG

Only a brave old maple,
   Shorn of its scarlet and gold,
And traced on the scroll of sunset
   As a hand-writing black and bold.

A low, wailing wind frets the branches ;
The dead leaves start up in surprise,
Till at length in the hush of the gloaming
The dryad's sad monody dies.

O desolate tree in the meadow,
With pleading hands stretched to the
   sky

Do you know the glad hopes of a spring-
    tide
Asleep in your folded arms lie?

And that never a breath of the Storm
    King,
And never a drift of the snow,
Can rifle the bud from its casket
Or loose the firm anchor below?

'Bide patiently, then, the bleak winter,
And change the sad wail to a song;
Bear up, for the robins and bluebirds
And South winds are coming, ere long!

———

An empty room! what could it mean?
Nay! could it be that under screen
Of night, and, mayhap, from the
    dread,
Of prison bars, that he had fled —
The British soldier? It is true
These convalescent weeks, they knew
How restlessly he paced the floor,
But then, they thought it nothing
    more
Than, in impatience, anyone

Recovering slowly might have done.
Yet here upon the table lay
His watch and purse — a note to say
This strange departure he could
    not
As yet, explain to any, but
Though words — deeds seemed in
    truth too rude
To show his fervent gratitude —
A debt to their sweet charity
The life they saved henceforth should
    be !

Silent and soft and white and slow —
On hill, stream, meadow — falls the
    snow.
A hush without, a hush within,
A cold drear world where all has
    been
So full of color, warmth, and glow ;
And Huldah — looking, listening —
    feels
A new strange loneliness that steals
The dimpling smile, the song half-
    way —
(As the bleak north winds chide and
    stay

With chilling breath and frowning
    look
The rippling laughter of the brook !)

And still with many a turn and phase
The fierce war spirit stirs and sways
The land that waits while Freedom's
    breath
Seems wavering 'twixt life and death.
The battles on the Jersey shore
And, now and then, the cannon's roar
From fleet and fort still keep alive
The patriot's hope, while bravely
    strive
The poor starved troops with Wash-
    ington —
A host himself ! — to spur them on.

Old Valley Forge — the story yet
Comes with fresh thrill, and eyes are
    wet
With tears unbid — what time we
    read
Of bitter suffering, bitter need,
All borne so uncomplainingly
By those whose eyes might never see
The boon they bought us — Liberty !

'Midst disappointment, ills untold —
Tories at home, and traitors bold,
With massacre at Wyoming
An added horror yet to bring!
Still, Burgoyne's late surrender fanned
To flame again hope's dying brand,
A flame that bright and brighter grew
When in Manhattan's harbor lay
At anchor, one glad summer day,
With pennons red and white and blue,
The long-expected, brave French fleet,
And Count D'Estaing commanding it.

O glad bright morning on the bay!
O sad, white dawning, as one ray —
One only — pierced the narrow slip
Of window, in the prison-ship —
The "*Jersey*" — worst of all through-
        out
The waters of the Wallabout!
Stifled and starved the prisoners lie
A wailing mass of misery,
And living sufferers envy those
Whose eyes are first in death to close.
O righteous Heaven! one day will
        show
Full justice to all men, we know;

But while the good still suffer wrong,
And weak hands writhe beneath the
    strong,
The cry must rise, " How long —
    how long ! "

Among the prisoners, one man
Creeps to the light, and dim eyes
    scan
With wistful look the harbor and
The long, low line of sea-girt land ;
How strange the bright blue water
    seems ! —
How cheerily the sunlight gleams
On snow-white sail, on sandy shore,
And fresh green turf where never-
    more
His feet may tread — and though
    the trace
Of suffering has aged his face,
It is — ah yes ! we know it now,
The kindling eye, the thoughtful
    brow
That Huldah kissed the morning
    when
The call had come for " minute-
    men."

Alas! how dim, how far away
It seems — that one short April day
When, hand to hand, he fought until
There came the sense of something
    chill
On hand and foot — a blank — and
    then
The British ambulances when
He woke and heard the questioning
    jeer,
" Why! how came such a rebel here?"
" We found him wounded in the road
And took him, since the 'red coat'
    showed
Our own, we thought — but, 'buff
    and blue'
A sturdier rebel never knew!"

" Ah well! they tried in vain to make
Me compromise, or base oath take!
And when they could not as a spy
Make use of me, they thought to try
Fresh cruelties and quite subdue
Me — but they little knew
The patriotic blood that flowed
Within my throbbing veins, and
    showed

The father, grandsire, who in strife
Of other days had yielded life
With hero spirit ! — Well — ah well !
They did their best, but could not
　　quell
My rebel ardor — years of pain,
Imprisonment — and what the gain ?
To fall were glorious on the field,
But this is pitiful — to yield
One's life by slow degrees, and know
That it is naught to friend or foe !
And yet if I could only see
The dear home faces, willingly
With my poor comrades they might
　　lay
Me down to rest — this very day ! "
So thought the prisoner as he heard,
" Bring out your dead ! " the morn-
　　ing word.

A hand upon the outer latch —
A closer crowding through the
　　hatch —
Who was it ? Some one else to
　　share
Their woe ? But no ! — the tall
　　form there —

" Good God ! it is the very face
I fought with in that narrow place
Beside the road!" and then he
    turned
To find conviction — all — con-
    firmed,
As pressing through the wailing
    crowd
The British soldier spoke aloud
His name, and grasping then his
    hand,
Without a greeting, said : " We
    stand —
Though in a very different place —
Once more, brave foe, face close to
    face !
We fought right well that April day,
But fiercest enemies, they say,
Make firmest friends — so may it be
Henceforward, Sir, with you and me !
For life itself, and far above
This breath of ours, the fire of
    love ! —
For all the sweetness of your home
A debtor to you I have come !
Yet never words of mine can tell
What bitter, bitter sorrow fell

That day when thinking of the face
I covered in that dreary place
With my own cloak, the knowledge
    came —
(It may have been the likeness there
In your sweet Huldah's brow and
    hair)
My foe — their loved one — 'tis the
    same!
Long months since then, now here,
    now there,
I've sought " the lost one " every-
    where,
For signed, you see, by our good
    king,
Your pardon and release I bring ! "

———

Five times the winter snows had lain
On field and river, upland, plain;
Now here, now there, the tide of war
North, South, East, West, alternate
    saw,
But hearts grew strong when helping
    hands
Were stretched from far-off foreign
    strands.

Pulaski, noble La Fayette,
And Kosciusko — even yet
Upon their generous deeds we dwell
And to our eager children tell.

Success, defeat — it was the same
Old tale — with just a change of
    name,
Until, one bright October morn
An unexpected joy was born;
And to its depths each patriot soul
Is stirred, while swift the tidings roll,
" Cornwallis has surrendered!   Ring
The bells in every town, and bring
The good news into every home —
To you and yours sweet Peace has
    come!"

And, ere the echoes die away,
Let us one short, swift moment stray
To Middlesex where field and brook —
The very farm yard — have a look
As if some sudden joy had come
To nestle in the hill-side home.
A sudden gust of wind that steals
The curtain from its place reveals,
Within the little " keeping room,"

(Most often doomed to cold and
    gloom!)
A lily here, a rosebud there,
Arranged with dainty thought and
    care,
And in their Sunday garments clad,
The merry lass, the bashful lad,
The dame with cap-box in her hand,
Come up the path, and now they
    stand
In quiet groups within; while two,
(A manly form with English face,
A girlish figure full of grace,
Yet freedom too, as if she knew
Her birthright!) joining hands re-
    peat
The promises, the pledges sweet —
" To love, to cherish — heart for
    heart —
In sickness, health — till Death us
    part!"

*Up from the meadows, down from the
    hills,*
*Snatched by the breezes, caught by the
    rills —*
    Hark! to the wonderful chorus!

*Warfare has ended in white truce of
    peace.
Jealousies, hatred, rivalries cease
  When Love her elixir breathes o'er
    us !*

*And still as the years with their
    changes roll by,
Breaking each barrier — strengthening
    each tie,
  Union grows stronger and stronger ;
Nation to nation is drawing more
    nigh —
And since of one language, aim, an-
    cestry, — why
  Should we cherish old enmities longer ?*

ESTHER'S DEFENCE
OF THE FORT

ESTHER'S DEFENCE OF THE FORT

A STORY OF ONE OF NEW HAMPSHIRE'S
DAUGHTERS

SINCE those far-off days when Mason
    came —
And Fernando Gorges of world-wide
    fame —
To found on Piscataqua's rockbound
    shore
A " Royal Province " (not only in
    name !)
With its sure, safe harbor and boun-
    teous store
Of nature's wealth in fish and game, —
New Hampshire's Daughters, stanch
    and strong,
Have left their record in story and
    song.

And those valiant deeds of the days
of old —
We never tire to hear them told,
When dangers threatened on every
hand
The lives and homes of that little
band
Of pioneers ! brave, patient, strong —
Unfading laurels to those belong
Who pushed their way through the
pathless wood,
Undaunted in faith and fortitude,
Till among the Granite Hills at
length
Rose their noble State in beauty and
strength !
And, helping always — a tireless
band ! —
Through the bye-gone years we see
them stand —
New Hampshire's Daughters, stanch
and strong,
Leaving their record in story and
song.

Brave Hannah Dustin ! — a shudder
and chill

Run through our frames and our
eyelids fill
As we read of her capture — the
dreadful fate
That awaited herself and her child
— the hate
Of the cruel, treacherous Indian
band
That at length lay slain by her own
right hand.

There was Mary Neff — there was
Molly Stark —
And many another of shining mark,
But among the names that are
handed down
From sire to son with their wide
renown,
Among the many I think of one
Who faced the enemy all alone !
A frail and slender woman, they said,
Was this Esther Jones with her clear,
wise head,
But she always knew what was best
to do —
That rare, fine gift bestowed on the
few.

And to Esther° it was, that every
    man
In the garrison came for the wisest
    plan
Of guiding the colony day by day
And keeping the savage tribes at
    bay —
For whatever she said they always
    knew
Was the best and the safest thing
    to do.

The planting, one spring, had been
    long delayed
Because of a treacherous Indian
    raid,
And when, at last, it could safely be
    done
If they worked together till set of
    the sun,
She bade all go and leave her on
    guard
In the garrison fort, well bolted and
    barred.

So, with loaded guns they had gone
    away —

Man, woman, and child from the
    fort that day, —
And Esther alone in the garrison
    stood,
Surrounded each side by the dense
    pine wood;
The nearest house was a mile away
And the savage tribes in ambush
    lay
Near the forest path, but she knew
    no fear —
This dauntless Esther who waited
    here.

The long, long day was nearing its
    close
When, suddenly, out on the still air
    rose
A wild war-whoop! —
                 Poor Esther knows
The wily foe at length have guessed
How weak is the fort! She must
    do her best —
She must rally all her wits to the
    front
For 'tis she alone who must bear the
    brunt

Of this savage horde. They are
　　coming fast
And she knows each moment may
　　be her last !

But, undismayed, she challenges all
The murderous host, and her figure
　　tall
Arrayed in her husband's coat and
　　hat
Looks now from this loop-hole, now
　　from that,
While with gun in hand they can
　　hear her call
To Peter, to John, to Henry, to
　　Paul,
And a host of others, as if there
　　stood
Beside her a stalwart brotherhood
Of valiant warriors !

　　　　　　With puzzled mien
The Indians pause — and while they
　　wait
As if hypnotized there by the gate
A troop of well-armed men is seen
Hemming them in on every side

While a panic seizes them far and
    wide.
The planting was over ere set of the
    sun
And an easy victory now is won !

Brave Esther Jones ! Till the day
    was done
Alone she had held the fort — among
New Hampshire's Daughters, stanch
    and strong,
Let her name be known in story and
    song !

MADAM HANCOCK'S RECEPTION

MADAM HANCOCK'S
RECEPTION

A HUNDRED years and more ago —
When haughty England was our
  foe —
In Boston harbor one bright day,
The brave French fleet at anchor lay.

And timely aid they gave us then —
The Count d'Estaing and all his
  men;
When hope from every heart had
  fled
And victories crowned the royal red.

"Now, ere to France they sail away,"
Said Hancock to his wife that day,
"For these good friends, so tried
  and true
In time of need — what can we do?"

Fair Dorothy with courtesy
And old-time hospitality,
Agreed at once to do her part
With ready hand and loyal heart : —

"For Count d'Estaing's brave staff,"
    she said,
" A fine French breakfast I will
    spread ;
A hearty welcome, right good cheer
Our generous allies shall find here ! "

. . . .

For thirty guests her board was laid
When   suddenly,   she   saw — dis-
    mayed —
The officers of *all* the fleet —
Eight-score and more, come down
    the street !

But with rare tact she swiftly threw
Her doors wide open, and none
    knew
Of all that crowd of gallant men
The lady's consternation when
She wondered how her larder's store
For *thirty* guests could feed *eight-
    score !*

Then came a sudden happy thought
As through the open door she caught
A glimpse of green where, in those
    days,
The neighbors' cows were wont to
    graze
On Boston Common; " Milk them
    all ! "
(She bade her servants) "and then
    call
At every house on Beacon Street
For food to feed our honored fleet."

And so it was that all were fed
Most sumptuously ; and each one
    said
That Madam with her gracious mien,
Had entertained them like a queen !

Then Count d'Estaing who would
    not be
Outdone in hospitality,
Begged Madam to invite some day
Her friends to meet them down the
    bay ;
And Madam (if the tale be true)
Invited all the friends she knew,

Till, in astonishment, the fleet
Five hundred Boston ladies greet !

But Count d'Estaing with beaming
    face
Received them all with courtly grace,
While *feu-de-joie* and cannonade
Old Boston Bay a fête-day made.

DORA

DORA

All Nature seemed awaking from her
    winter nap ;
The trees, though leafless, felt the
    rising sap
Stir in their veins ; the robin's clarion
    call
Rang out upon the morning air, and
    all
The strange, sweet restlessness of
    Spring seemed given
Within the blue-bird's note ; bright
    smiled the heaven,
And, patiently, the fresh-ploughed
    earth beneath
Was waiting Nature's miracle ; a
    wreath
Of curling smoke from briar and
    brushwood rose
To be again incarnate — but who
    knows
In what new form of life ?

Beside the door —
The open door that looks o'er
    wood and moor —
Dora, the farmer's daughter, stands
    that day ;
And blushes with the merry dimples
    play
Upon her cheeks, as, suddenly, she
    sees
A hurrying form among the orchard
    trees ;
And now within the door young
    Ezra stands —
Ezra, the neighbor's son, whose sun-
    burnt hands
Are filled with flowers ; arbutus
    buds he brings,
Hepaticas, anemones — the Spring's
First gifts, and as he lets them fall
Into her hands, he whispers in her
    ear —
(Fond lover's words for no one else
    to hear) —
That she is fairer, sweeter than them
    all ! —
But now there comes a quick, excited
    call,

" Hist ! Dora, Ezra ! ere to-morrow's
    sun
The red-coats will be here from Lex-
    ington ! "
Aud Dora's father bids them swift
    conceal
In fresh-ploughed earth, in barrels,
    bags of meal,
The ammunition he had brought the
    day
Before, from neighboring towns to
    store away
For future need.

    And then, to Dora, came
A sudden inspiration, as a flame
Of patriot ardor fired her breast —
One place there was the British in
    their quest
Would never think to search, or if
    they did
The bullets and the powder could be
    hid
Securely 'neath the linen in her
    chest —
The wedding chest where she had
    laid away

'Mongst bags of fragrant lavender
that day
Her homespun outfit, for no foreign
gown
Was worn by maid or matron in the
town
Of "red-hot" rebel fame!
The very name
Of buying English taffeta, a
shame —
A "tory" act was deemed, and for
their tea
They dried the raspberry leaves that
all might see
How odious was the "Stamp" of
tyranny!

So, Dora's wedding garments, every
one
Was made from wool and flax her
hands had spun,
And woven on the home-made wheel
and loom,
And laid within the coffer in her
room —
The quaint, carved oaken coffer, worn
and brown,

Through many generations, handed
    down
Yet strong as any miser's chest.

                       Meanwhile,
From Lincoln, Acton, Chelmsford
    and Carlisle,
And all the neighboring towns came
    minute-men —
Plain, sturdy farmers, but brave
    fighters when
The conflict came, as every school-
    boy knows!

Within the woods, in hay-lofts, fields,
    they chose
The safest places they could find to
    hide
Their precious ammunition; far and
    wide
They scattered it throughout old
    Concord town
Before the British red-coats had
    come down
From Lexington; but spite of all
    their care

Five hundred pounds of balls were
  captured where
They thought them most secure.

                    To Dora's home
By seven o'clock a hungry band had
  come,
And mindful how in Holy Writ we
  read
That even our worst foes we still
  should feed,
The mother, like a Christian, opened
  wide
Her larder doors, but when the
  British tried
To make some payment, " Nay ! "
  she proudly cried,
" Take back your price of blood ! "
  With rude haste, then,
The house was searched and sacked
  throughout ; but when
Sweet Dora's room was reached, the
  red-coats said —
(An insolent young captain at their
  head !)
" Give us a kiss, my pretty maid,
  and we

Will not disturb your wedding
   finery ! "

Then, furious at her cold, disdainful
   mien,
The soldiers broke the quaint, old
   carven chest
And slashed the dainty garments in
   their quest,
But ere they found the bullets hid
   between,
A sudden shot upon the bridge was
   heard.
And hurriedly they seized — each
   man — his sword
And gun, and hastened at their cap-
   tain's word
To hold the entrance of the old
   North bridge,
For minute-men were seen upon the
   ridge
And messengers were at the door to
   tell
How, there, the two rash red-coat
   troopers fell !

Ah ! what a strange, uncanny day it
   seemed ! —

Poor Dora walked about as one who
 dreamed;
Her wedding garments ruined past
 repair
She put again within the coffer
 where
The powder and the bullets still lay
 hid;
When Ezra came to say good-bye,
 she bid
Him " God-speed " with a calm,
 strong face
That of her aching heart showed not
 a trace,
" It is a glorious cause for which you
 fight
To-day," she said, " I would we
 women might
Do more than wish you well, but we
 alas !
Can only wait and pray while slowly
 pass
The long, long weary hours ! " and
 Dora saw
As in a vision how the tide of war
Which rose that April day would
 sweep ere long

Through all the land with current
    fierce and strong,
And claim, as sacrifice, full many a
    life
Ere victory, at last, might crown the
    strife.

But Ezra, thinking of the wedding
    day,
With all a lover's hopefulness could
    say,
" 'Tis only for a little while, dear
    heart, —
Surely I shall be back again ere
    long,
And you, sweet one, so steadfast,
    brave and strong
Will not despond although to-day
    we part."
And so with kiss and clasp they said
    good-bye
And Ezra hastened down the road
    to try
The rusty flint-lock that his grand-
    sire bore
In French and Indian wars, long
    years before.

    .   .   .   .

"A little while?" Six times the
    flowers of May
Had bloomed and faded since that
    parting day.
Six, long, heroic years of bitter strife
    had passed
Before sweet Liberty was won at
    last.
"Peace— Liberty, at last!" the hap-
    py bells ring on
Until they reach the home where
    Dora spun
And wove her wedding garments
    long ago —
Fair wedding garments white as
    driven snow.
Through door, through window
    streams the autumn sun
And from the maple bough that
    sweeps the sill,
Blood-red the leaves have fallen.

    Grave and still
Yet holding in her eyes a wondrous
    light —
As if she saw some far-off radiant
    sight —

A black-robed woman gathers up the
    leaves
And looks far out across the harvest
    sheaves
To church and churchyard where the
    sunbeams cast
Long shadows on a grassy mound —
    the last
Low bivouac !— and yet, why should
    she weep ?
Sweet is the victory won, and sweet
    the victor's sleep !